Ruth

30 Biblical Insights by **Sim Kay Tee**

Journey Through Ruth
© 2019 by Sim Kay Tee
All rights reserved.

Discovery House is affiliated
with Our Daily Bread Ministries.

Requests for permission to quote
from this book should be directed to:

Permissions Department
Discovery House
P.O. Box 3566
Grand Rapids, MI 49501

Or contact us by email at
permissionsdept@dhp.org

Scriptures taken from Holy Bible, New International Version® Anglicized, NIV®
Copyright © 1973, 1978, 1984, 2011 by Biblica, Inc®. Used by permission.
All rights reserved worldwide.

Design by Joshua Tan
Typeset by Grace Goh

ISBN 978-1-913135-05-8

Printed in the United Kingdom
Second Printing in 2019

Foreword

The book of Ruth itself does not indicate who the author is, but Talmudic traditions say it was the prophet Samuel.[1] Since the genealogy mentions only David and not Solomon (Ruth 4:22), some scholars believe that Samuel wrote this book after anointing David as king (1 Samuel 16:1–13, circa 1025 BC).[2]

Most scholars, however, believe that David was already king at the time of writing, and that since Samuel died five years before David was crowned (25:1; 2 Samuel 2:1–4), he could not have written it. These scholars believe that Ruth was written by an unnamed royal chronicler or scribe during the reign of David (circa 1010–970 BC).[3] The story of Ruth is thus an ancient one.

The book recounts the humble beginnings of David, Israel's greatest and most-loved king, showing how God providentially followed his ancestors and sovereignly shepherded their lives. It also shows how God used Ruth to perpetuate the messianic line, as the great-grandmother of King David and ancestor of Jesus (Ruth 4:17; Matthew 1:1–6). The book of Ruth thus celebrates God's sovereign plan, power, providence, protection, and provision.

That Ruth, a despised Moabitess, became an ancestor of Jesus is also revealing (1:1, 5). Through Ruth, God was already declaring to the world that Gentiles are included in Christ's redemptive work (Ephesians 3:6). Jesus is not just the Jewish Messiah, but "the Saviour of the world" (John 4:42; 1 John 4:14).

Dedicated to Lay Keng, the love of my life.

Soli Deo gloria,
Sim Kay Tee

---

[1] Rabbinic tradition as cited by Crossway Bibles, "Introduction to Ruth", in *ESV Study Bible* (Wheaton, IL: Crossway Bibles, 2008), 473.

[2] The anointing of David was circa 1025 BC. See Tyndale House Publishers, "Introduction to 1 Samuel", in *NLT Study Bible* (Carol Stream, IL: Tyndale House Publishers, 2008), 465.

[3] David ruled Israel 1010–970 BC. See Kenneth Barker, ed., "Introduction: 1 Samuel", in *NIV Study Bible* (Grand Rapids, MI: Zondervan, 1985), 373.

We're glad you've decided to join us on a journey into a deeper relationship with Jesus Christ!

For over 50 years, we have been known for our daily Bible reading notes, *Our Daily Bread*. Many readers enjoy the pithy, inspiring, and relevant articles that point them to God and the wisdom and promises of His unchanging Word.

Building on the foundation of *Our Daily Bread*, we have developed this devotional series to help believers spend time with God in His Word, book by book. We trust this daily meditation on God's Word will draw you into a closer relationship with Him through our Lord and Saviour, Jesus Christ.

How to use this resource

READ: This book is designed to be read alongside God's Word as you journey with Him. It offers explanatory notes to help you understand the Scriptures in fresh ways.

REFLECT: The questions are designed to help you respond to God and His Word, letting Him change you from the inside out.

RECORD: The space provided allows you to keep a diary of your journey as you record your thoughts and jot down your responses.

An Overview

The story of Ruth involves two people who are worlds apart—ethnically, culturally, and economically. Ruth is a poor young Moabite widow who has followed Naomi, her aged mother-in-law, back to Israel, trying her utmost to survive in a foreign land. Boaz is a wealthy landowner and highly respected Israelite from Bethlehem. He is a relative, a guardian-redeemer of Elimelek (Ruth 2:20), Naomi's late husband. Boaz is much older than Ruth (3:10–11).

As affection and then love grows between Boaz and Ruth, a wedding is anticipated. But there is a problem: the prevailing custom on levirate marriage gives the nearest relative the first right to marry Ruth (Deuteronomy 25:5–10), and Boaz is only second in line (Ruth 3:12–13). If the nearest relative exercises his right, Boaz and Ruth cannot be together.

However, God has declared that "the sceptre will not depart from Judah" (Genesis 49:10), the tribe to which Boaz belongs (Matthew 1:3–5). One of his descendants will be the King to whom all nations will submit and give honour (1:16). God will ensure that this comes to pass, saying: "Surely, as I have planned, so it will be, and as I have purposed, so it will happen" (Isaiah 14:24).

The story of Ruth is about how God works in and through the ordinary circumstances of life. There are no spectacular signs and wonders to showcase. The characters of the story are common, ordinary folks in an everyday setting, struggling with bread and butter issues, trying to raise a family in a morally-corrupt and godless world (Ruth 1:1).

But God's resolute—albeit invisible—hand is directing such people to accomplish His divine purposes and plans. And whenever and wherever God works, it is extraordinary, miraculous, and divine!

Key Verse
"Where you go I will go, and where you stay I will stay. Your people will be my people and your God my God." —Ruth 1:16

Day 1

Read Ruth 1:1–2

I was at the airport recently to bid farewell to an old classmate who was moving with his family to another country. Left without work for more than a year, he eventually found a job in a city known for its opposition to the Christian faith. But the pay was good, he reasoned, and his children only needed to be there for two years.

The story of Ruth starts with Elimelek making the difficult decision to relocate his family to Moab. It has become impossible to put food on the table because of a famine in the land (Ruth 1:1). Elimelek lives "in the days when the judges ruled" (1:1). We are not told when exactly this was within the 300-year period (about 1380–1050 BC)[4] between the death of Joshua (Joshua 24:29) and the beginning of Saul's reign as king (1 Samuel 13:1). But we know that this was a treacherous time. It was characterised by political instability, decadent immorality, and spiritual idolatry; it was a time when "everyone did as they saw fit" (Judges 17:6; 21:25). God's people had turned from Him to worship idols (2:10–13; 3:5–6).

God had warned that if His people were unfaithful, He would discipline them by sending famine on the land (Deuteronomy 11:16–17). That "the LORD had come to the aid of his people by providing food for them" later on (Ruth 1:6) hints that this famine was God's punishment for their unfaithfulness (Leviticus 26:18–20; Amos 4:6–9).

Elimelek, whose name means "God is my king", ironically does not acknowledge God as King. He has not accepted God's disciplining hand through the famine. If he had, the appropriate response would have been repentance, not relocation (Deuteronomy 30:1–3). Instead of repenting, calling on God for mercy, and trusting Him to provide food in the Promised Land, Elimelek designs his own solution. Moving his whole family to Moab, however, will prove to be a poor decision.

How strange that there should be a famine in Bethlehem, for Bethlehem means "house of bread". On the other hand, God called Moab "my washbasin" (Psalm 108:9). The residual filth from washing makes the washbasin an object of mockery and contempt. Metaphorically, Elimelek is leaving "the house of bread" for a wasteland, a garbage dump!

Major decisions in life cannot be based entirely on economic or financial considerations. Spiritual considerations are imperative. Moab may be a good place to put bread on the table, but it is not conducive to living a holy life or raising godly children. Moab may offer material sustenance, even worldly success, but it is a hindrance to spiritual growth, a threat to spiritual survival.

⁴ Barker, "Introduction to Judges", *NIV Study Bible*, 326.

If you have to put food on the table, would you decide differently from Elimelek? What are some important considerations that would affect your decision?

Have you, like Elimelek, left Bethlehem (moved out of God's will) to go to Moab, a dirty "washbasin" (Psalm 108:9)? Isn't it time to return home?

Day 2

Read Ruth 1:3–5

A modern-day parable tells of a frog being slowly boiled alive. The premise is that if the frog is put suddenly into boiling water, it will jump out of harm's way immediately. But if the frog is put into tepid water that is then slowly brought to a boil, it will not perceive the danger. The frog will acclimatise to the increasing temperature until it is cooked to death.

Not long after moving to Moab, Naomi becomes a widow (Ruth 1:3). Things have not turned out the way she hoped. Widowed and alone, she now has to raise her two boys in a foreign land all by herself. The logical solution is for her to return to the Promised Land immediately.

Instead of heading home, Naomi remains in Moab. Elimelek and Naomi intended to live in Moab "for a while" (1:1), but it turns out to be a substantial "ten years" (1:4). Their temporal sojourn has become permanent residency. Settled down in Moab, her two sons marry Moabite women (1:4; 4:10).

God had commanded the Jews not to marry people from the neighbouring nations: "Do not intermarry with them. Do not give your daughters to their sons or take their daughters for your sons, for they will turn your children away

from following me to serve other gods" (Deuteronomy 7:3–4, see also Exodus 34:15–16). Moabite women were reputed to be immoral and idolatrous (Numbers 25:1–2). Imagine the spiritual and moral quagmire Naomi found herself in. Idolatrous and permissive, Moabite culture was not the environment to raise children in (Nehemiah 13:23–26). **You take on the values of the culture you live in.**

Ten years later, both Mahlon and Kilion also died, leaving Naomi "without her two sons and her husband" (Ruth 1:5). This signals the tragic end of the Elimelek family line. In ancient Jewish society, a woman's sense of security and dignity was tied to her husband and sons. Naomi is now devoid of any descendants and thus security; an heirless widow is the epitome of the hopeless poor. She has no hope for the future of her family. If Elimelek's family name is to carry on, there needs to be an heir.

As for the deaths of the three men, we can only surmise why they died, for the Bible does not tell us. Jewish tradition says their deaths were God's punishment for their sins—Elimelek for leaving the Promised Land, and Mahlon and Kilion for marrying

Moabites. That the two sons were married for 10 years without fathering any children also points to the disciplining hand of God. A barren womb is among the list of covenantal curses (Deuteronomy 28:15, 18).

The story begins with tragedy. This family makes a bad decision and exchanges one famine for three funerals. All that is left of the once-complete family are three widows—Naomi and her two daughters-in-law, Ruth and Orpah. But no male heir.

If you were Naomi, would you allow your children to marry people of a different ethnicity and culture? Would you stop them from marrying those of different religious affiliations (Ruth 1:4)? Why or why not?

What are the benefits and dangers of assimilating the values of the community we live in? How can we ensure that we adopt the good and avoid the bad?

Day 3

Read Ruth 1:6–7

"Every cloud has a silver lining" is a proverb that is often used to encourage a person whose chips are down. One wonders how many times Naomi heard this during those difficult years in Moab—that even in the midst of tragedy and despair, there is the prospect of better things to come.

Indeed, the silver lining does appear for Naomi. There is good news! Sometime after the death of her two sons, Naomi hears that there is now food in Bethlehem. The famine in Judah, which has lasted more than 10 years (Ruth 1:1, 4), is finally over. The weather has changed and the rains have come, nourishing the fertile land to produce a bountiful harvest. The reason given for the availability of food, however, is not agrarian but theological. It is not so much that the rains have come; rather, it is that "the LORD [has] come to the aid of his people" (1:6; see Leviticus 26:3–5). When His people turned to Him for deliverance, God "remembered his covenant and out of his great love he relented" and withdrew His disciplining hand (Psalm 106:43–45). Interestingly, the Targum (the ancient Aramaic paraphrase of the Hebrew Bible) says that the famine ended because of the merit and the petitionary prayer of the judge "Ibzan of Bethlehem", fourth of the six minor judges (Judges 12:8), whom the Rabbis identify with Boaz.[5]

That it takes the Israelites more than 10 years to return to God tells us something about how rebelliously stubborn and stiff-necked they are (Deuteronomy 9:6, 13; 31:27). They would rather suffer than repent. What is true of them may well be true of us, too. **Often, we are quick to sin but extremely slow to repent.** We ask for deliverance without repentance.

Reversing the direction she and Elimelek had taken, "[Naomi] and her daughters-in-law [prepare] to return home from there" (Ruth 1:6). Bible teacher Warren Wiersbe astutely observes: "Naomi's decision was right, but her motive was wrong. She was still interested primarily in food, not in fellowship with God. She was returning to her land but not to her Lord".[6]

The good news Naomi hears is that "the LORD had come to the aid of his people by providing food for them" (1:6). The expression "by providing food" in Hebrew literally means "gave them bread".[7] Is this not the same good news we have today? God has come to our rescue, giving us "the true bread from heaven" (John 6:32). To all who are spiritually

Why do you think it took the Israelites so long (10 years) to repent?

Would you agree that often, we are quick to sin but extremely slow to repent? Why or why not? How can we become more sensitive to sin in our lives?

hungry, Jesus extends this invitation: "I am the bread of life. Whoever comes to me will never go hungry" (6:35). Perhaps, like Naomi, we just need to return home to the Lord.

[5] Tamara Cohn Eskenazi and Tikva Frymer-Kensky, *The JPS Bible Commentary: Ruth*, first edition, JPS Tanakh Commentary (Philadelphia, PA: Jewish Publication Society, 2011), 8.
[6] Warren W. Wiersbe, *Be Committed*, "Be" Commentary Series (Wheaton, IL: Victor Books, 1993), 18.
[7] Jan de Waard and Eugene Albert Nida, *A Translator's Handbook on the Book of Ruth*, 2nd edition, UBS Handbook Series (New York: United Bible Societies, 1991), 10.

Day 4

Read Ruth 1:8–10

No relationship is more irksome than that between in-laws. Conflicts often plague the marital relationship because mother-in-law and daughter-in-law cannot get along. Although Naomi's spiritual health at this time is at its lowest (see Ruth 1:13, 20–21), her relationship with her daughters-in-law is at its height. Remarkably, Naomi is a good mother-in-law who enjoys a close and endearing relationship with her two daughters-in-law. Perhaps their painful shared experience as widows has drawn them even closer. When Naomi sets out to return to Bethlehem, Ruth and Orpah follow her (1:6–7). Maybe they feel duty-bound, but more likely they have become so devoted to their mother-in-law that they are willing to leave Moab to care for the elderly Naomi.

On the way back to Bethlehem, Naomi has a change of heart. Concerned for their safety and welfare, she urges Ruth and Orpah not to leave the familiarity and security of their Moabite home for Bethlehem—where they will almost certainly be rejected and ostracised.

The Moabites, who were descended from Lot through an incestuous union with his older daughter (Genesis 19:30–38), were long-time enemies of the Israelites (Numbers 22–25). When the Israelites were making their way into the Promised Land, Moabite women seduced the Israelite men and led them into idolatry, causing them to sin against the Lord. Eventually, 24,000 Israelites died by God's disciplining hand (Numbers 25:1–9).

Because they had mistreated and harmed the Israelites, the Moabites were not allowed to enter the temple to worship God (Deuteronomy 23:3; Nehemiah 13:1–3). God also ordered the Jews not to seek "a treaty of friendship with them as long as you live" (Deuteronomy 23:6). During the period of the judges, the Israelites were subject to the Moabite king Eglon for 18 years (Judges 3:14). Given their long history of hostility and enmity, no Israelite would welcome a Moabite into their midst.

And so Naomi encourages her daughters-in-law to remain in Moab and start new families for themselves (Ruth 1:9), bidding them goodbye. **She believes they have a better future in Moab, for Jews are not allowed to "promote the welfare and prosperity of the . . . Moabites" (Deuteronomy 23:6 NLT).**

But Orpah and Ruth are undeterred. Despite knowing that they face an uncertain future in Bethlehem, they stick to their decision: "We will go back with you" (Ruth 1:10). Their willingness to give up family and friends, their future and their happiness, shows their devotion to their mother-in-law.

Would you agree or disagree with Naomi that both Ruth and Orpah have a better future in Moab? Why or why not?

If you have to live in a community that is unwelcoming of Christianity, what are some challenges or dangers this may pose to your Christian faith?

Day 5

In many patriarchal societies, parents favour sons over daughters. This favouritism also runs deep in Jewish culture. Sons perpetuate the family line, while daughters marry out to carry on the line of their husbands' families. Patriarchal societies are also patrilineal—family property and titles are inherited only by the male line. The Old Testament allows daughters to inherit family property, only if there are no male heirs. These daughters must then marry within the tribal clan of their fathers to keep the property within the tribe (see Numbers 27:1–11; 36:5–9).

Levirate marriage is an arrangement prescribed by Mosaic Law in which a man is required to marry the widow of his brother who dies with no male heir (Deuteronomy 25:5–10). The term "levirate", from the Latin word *levir*, means "husband's brother". The intent of this law is to provide an heir for the dead brother to continue his family line. The law is also designed to take care of the widow. Levirate marriage forms the backdrop of the story of Judah, his son Onan, and his daughter-in-law Tamar (Genesis 38:6–30). It is also the backdrop of the book of Ruth. And it is on the mind of Naomi: she tries to persuade her daughters-in-law to return to Moab because levirate marriage is no longer an option for them.

Naomi is not exactly thrilled by their renewed resolve to follow her to Bethlehem (Ruth 1:10). She is too old to provide them with new husbands to replace her dead sons, and therefore they have no future if they remain with her. Twice more she pushes them away: "Return home . . . return home" (1:11–12). However, instead of acknowledging that her dire situation is the result of her family's poor decision to leave the Promised Land, Naomi blames God, saying, "the Lord's hand has turned against me!" Far from being broken and repentant before God, Naomi is bitter towards Him (1:13).

One would expect Naomi to want to bring her two pagan daughters-in-law to the Promised Land, to know Yahweh, the true God. Instead, she is bent on sending them back to their idolatrous way of life (1:15). She succeeds with one: convinced, and tearfully parting ways with Naomi, Orpah takes the road back to Moab, to worship "Chemosh the detestable god of Moab" (1:15; 1 Kings 11:7). Sadly, Orpah returns to a lost destiny! But Ruth, undeterred, "clung to [Naomi]" (Ruth 1:14).

Why would Naomi, who knows the true God, hinder two pagan women from coming to follow Him?

Theories abound. Bible commentator Warren Wiersbe suggests that "Naomi didn't want to take Orpah and Ruth to Bethlehem because they were living proof that she and her husband had permitted their two sons to marry women from outside the covenant nation. In other words, Naomi was trying to cover up her disobedience."[8]

[8] Wiersbe, *Be Committed*, 19.

Think about Naomi's reasoning for why Ruth and Orpah should not return to the Promised Land with her (Ruth 1:11–13). In what ways is it valid or invalid?

In what ways can our words or actions hinder or deter someone from seeking the truth about God?

Day 6

Read Ruth 1:14–18

One of the more popular songs to come out of the 1992 movie *Sister Act* was the song "I Will Follow Him"—the movie's closing chorus item performed by a group of nuns. Originally a 1963 chart-topping song about a teenager's love for her boyfriend, actress Whoopi Goldberg and the nuns added a twist to it, turning it into a song about religious faith and devotion. The devotion and affection expressed in the song would certainly resonate with Ruth as she tearfully assures her mother-in-law, uttering these now-famous words: "Where you go I will go, and where you stay I will stay. Your people will be my people and your God my God" (Ruth 1:16).

Unlike Orpah, Ruth does not succumb to Naomi's dismal portrayal of her future prospects in Bethlehem (1:14). In a last-ditch effort to get Ruth off her back, Naomi pleads, "Look, Ruth, your sister-in-law has made the better and wiser choice. You need to follow her example and go back to worshipping your god Chemosh!" (see 1:15). Tragically, Naomi believes the gods of Moab can do more for Ruth than the God of Israel! Ironically, Ruth, a Moabitess, has more faith in Israel's God than Naomi herself.

We are not told how Ruth came to know about Yahweh, or how much she knows about Him. Perhaps Naomi, despite her present lack of faith, has positively influenced Ruth somewhat. We have seen how devoted her daughters-in-law are to her. Naomi must have told them how the Lord had rescued the Jews from slavery, given them a land, and made them into a nation. Ruth knows enough to want to worship this God of the Jews instead of the gods of Moab. Facing the most important decision of her life, and despite the persuasion and pressure not to believe, Ruth "[turns] to God from idols to serve the living and true God" (1 Thessalonians 1:9). **This passage is Ruth's conversion story.**

"Where you go I will go, and where you stay I will stay. Your people will be my people and your God my God" (Ruth 1:16). This verse has become the classic Christian expression of devotion and loyalty. Despite knowing that she will outlive Naomi by many years and will be alone in a foreign land after Naomi passes on, Ruth makes an irrevocable lifetime commitment to remain in Bethlehem, sealing it with an oath in the name of "the LORD" (YHWH or Yahweh in Hebrew), the covenantal name of God (1:17). She even invokes curses on herself if she ever reneges on her commitment. What determination!

One Bible teacher notes that Lot, the ancestor of Ruth (Genesis 19:36–37), had wilfully chosen to live outside the Promised Land (13:11–12). His descendant Ruth now reverses this decision, wilfully choosing to die inside God's Land. For the ancients, the land you were buried in indicated where your heart and real home lay (e.g. Joshua 24:30, 32). Naomi is not the only one going back home. For Ruth, Bethlehem will now be her true home (Ruth 1:17).

ThinkThrough

How can we be sure that Ruth believes in Yahweh (Ruth 1:16–17)?

Consider your own prayer of commitment when you first believed and embraced Jesus as your Lord and Saviour. What did you pray? Since then, have you settled in with a home church?

Day 7

Read Ruth 1:19–22

Age-progression technology helps investigators solve crimes and find missing persons. This innovative software has also been used to predict what individuals will look like in the future, modelling the effects of lifestyle habits such as drinking, smoking, diet, exercise, and stress. If applied to Naomi, this software would show that the painful trials of her life have taken their toll on her, making her look older than she really is.

As Naomi and Ruth enter Bethlehem, "the whole town [is] stirred because of them" (Ruth 1:19). Bethlehem is a small town (Micah 5:2), and the people will have remembered Naomi even after so long. But their question, "Can this be Naomi?" (Ruth 1:19), suggests they barely recognise her. Her appearance has been considerably and conspicuously altered by suffering.

The Bible tells of people who were renamed to reflect their changed circumstances (e.g. Genesis 32:28; 35:18; Daniel 1:7). The childless Abram and Sarai became Abraham and Sarah to reflect how they would have countless descendants (Genesis 17:5, 15). Naomi's parents had given her a beautiful name, meaning "sweetness or pleasantness". Perhaps that was the character trait that drew her daughters-in-law to her.

But now, Naomi asks to be renamed "Mara" to reflect her harsh life (Ruth 1:20). She blames God for her plight: "The Almighty has made my life very bitter . . . the Almighty has brought misfortune upon me" (1:20–21).

Is Naomi wrong, sacrilegious even, to accuse God like that? Perhaps not. Naomi uses the title, "the Almighty" (Hebrew *Shaddai*, "the All-Powerful One"), that God himself used when He appeared to Abraham and Jacob promising great covenantal abundance; only He had the power to fulfil such promises (e.g. Genesis 17:1; 35:11).[9] In calling God "the Almighty", Naomi acknowledges His sovereign dealings in her life; that the tragedies were not accidents, but God's hand had been in each of them. Now, back in the Promised Land, notwithstanding her downcast look, she commits her remaining days to "El Shaddai", trusting Him to fulfil His covenantal promises.

In saying that God has made "[her] life very bitter" (Ruth 1:20), Naomi is demonstrating "a freedom of a faith" that enables her to speak with raw honesty.[10] Naomi is not the first believer to do so. Hundreds of years earlier, the patriarch Job was even more pointed. "God has wronged me," he said, accusing God of injustice (Job 19:6). The psalmists, too, spoke directly to God with the same uninhibited candour (Psalm 22:1–2; 38:1–3; 42:9–10; 90:7; 102:10).

These Scriptures suggest that in our suffering, God invites us to direct our heartfelt disappointment and even anger towards Him. Complaints directed at God, as opposed to complaints about God to others, are therapeutically and spiritually good for our souls. There is room for us to bare our souls, and tell God honestly how we feel about Him. After all, He already knows us intimately (139:4).

Naomi's return ends her journey of bad decisions and disobedience. That "the barley harvest was beginning" (Ruth 1:22) marks a new beginning for her, and potentially good things to come. She will soon find out that one of God's richest blessings for her is her daughter-in-law, Ruth.

⁹ Warren Baker and Eugene Carpenter, *Complete Word Study Dictionary: Old Testament* (Chattanooga, TN: AMG, 2003), s.v. "H7706".
¹⁰ Fredric W. Bush, *Ruth–Esther*, vol. 9, Word Biblical Commentary (Dallas, TX: Word, 1998), 95–96.

Did Naomi sin when she blamed God for making her life bitter and miserable (Ruth 1:20–21)? Why or why not? Why would you agree or disagree that God invites us to direct our frustrations in life towards Him?

Who in your life is like Ruth, loyal to you in your painful trials? How can you be like Ruth to someone else in their time of need and distress?

Day 8

Read Ruth 2:1–3

Most civilised societies have welfare programmes to help feed the poor. In giving the Israelites "a land flowing with milk and honey" (Leviticus 20:24), God also commanded them to take care of the poor living among them (19:9–10; 23:22; Deuteronomy 24:19–22). They were to deliberately not harvest everything so that the needy could glean the leftovers to feed themselves, working for their food with a modicum of dignity. **God's solution to hungry stomachs involves the generous hearts and open hands of His people (Deuteronomy 15:4–11).**

In the days when judges ruled (Ruth 1:1), and "everyone did as they saw fit" (Judges 17:6), unscrupulous landowners would not allow the poor to glean. As a woman and foreigner living in perilous times (Ruth 2:2, see 2:9, 22), Ruth hopes to "go to the fields and pick up the leftover grain behind anyone in whose eyes I find favour" (or "grace", 2:2 KJV). We are not told how she knows of this Mosaic provision, but this tells us that since marrying a Jew, Ruth has taken the trouble to learn more about God and His laws. Ruth volunteers to glean. Naomi? Perhaps she is too old—or too proud—to glean. This is a step of faith for Ruth, for it means she not only believes what God says, and is also acting upon it (James 2:17). Relying on His grace, Ruth is trusting

God to protect and to provide.

Her choice of field is random. But "as it [turns] out", Ruth finds herself working in a field belonging to Boaz, a wealthy and influential relative from the clan of Elimelek (Ruth 2:1, 3). One rabbinic tradition says Boaz was a nephew of Elimelek,[11] though Scripture does not define what the precise relationship was. A chance occurrence? This "happenstance" is God's mysterious providence working through the ordinary circumstances of life.

Boaz is "a man of standing" (in Hebrew, *'is gibbor hayil*). The same description is used of Gideon and Jephthah, each of whom was called a "mighty warrior" (Judges 6:12; 11:1). Given that these are the perilous times of the judges, Boaz could well be a military leader too. Perhaps that is why the Talmud identifies him as the minor judge Ibzan (12:8).[12] There were two pillars at the portico of Solomon's temple, named Jakin (meaning "He establishes") and Boaz (meaning "in Him is strength", see NIV footnotes for 1 Kings 7:21; 2 Chronicles 3:17). Some scholars say this was to remind the Israelites that it is the Almighty God who established the Davidic throne. Others surmised that these pillars, named after two of Solomon's ancestors, were to affirm that Boaz was a key person in the ancestry of David.

[11] Note on Ruth 2:1–7 in Thomas L. Constable, "Constable's Notes", Lumina, accessed 21 September 2018, https://lumina.bible.org/bible/Ruth+2.
[12] Note on Ruth 2:1 in J. Gordon Harris, Cheryl A. Brown, and Michael S. Moore, *Joshua, Judges, Ruth*, Understanding the Bible Commentary Series (Grand Rapids, MI: Baker Books, 2012).

The law of gleaning is God's care for the poor (Leviticus 19:9–10; 23:22; Deuteronomy 24:19–22). How can Christians today apply this law to help the poor in our midst?

What welfare programme does your home church have for helping the poor and the needy in the community? What is one thing you can do to help the poor on a regular basis?

Day 9

Read Ruth 2:4–7

According to two 2017 regional surveys involving some eight economies, almost half of all workers in Singapore were unhappy because of issues with their bosses. Is it surprising, then, that workers in Singapore are the least engaged in Asia?[13] The kind of boss we have affects our work attitude. Perhaps having awful bosses contributes to Monday morning blues?

As Ruth is gleaning, Boaz comes into his fields to see the progress of the barley harvest. "Just then" (Ruth 2:4) indicates divine providence and timing, for the simultaneous arrivals of Ruth and Boaz are no coincidence.

Uncharacteristic of landowners of the time, Boaz greets his workers first, giving us an immediate insight into his character—a godly and humble man of benevolent disposition. Instead of the typical "Peace, shalom", Boaz's "the LORD be with you!" (2:4) tells us that he is one of those who believe that their faith in God should show in their daily work. Faith in God is active and real in Boaz's life. How many of us have our bosses greeting us first, and blessing us this manner? The workers warmly reciprocate, showing us how much they respect and love their boss.

Boaz takes notice of the strangers and poor who have come into his fields to glean. Concerned for these gleaners, he asks about Ruth (2:5). Once again we are reminded, "She is the Moabite who came back from Moab with Naomi" (2:6). Notice how the foreman stresses her foreignness!

Although the law gives her the right to glean, Ruth does not presume so. As an alien, she knows she has no claim on anyone. Instead, she has respectfully asked for permission to gather the leftover grain (2:7).

In recovering from a prolonged famine, landowners are apt to harvest everything, not allowing any gleaners to come into their fields. But the foreman knows that Boaz will agree to the poor, even a foreigner like Ruth, gleaning in his fields. He does not chase her away. Even as she looks to God to provide, Ruth does her part, for the foreman notices that she has worked diligently, "from morning till now, except for a short rest" (2:6–7). What the foreman says of Ruth speaks of her character—courteous, respectful, and diligent.

Two different persons, each on opposite sides of the economic and social spectrum. Boaz the wealthy, influential Israelite landowner, Ruth the destitute Moabite widow. **But both demonstrate a common characteristic: faith in God is real and active in their lives.**

Both know of God's laws, and both obediently act on them. Both seek to live a godly life. And as the story unfolds, their respect for each other increases, and so does love.

[13] Angela Teng, "Survey finds 45% of S'poreans unhappy at work in 2017", *TODAY*, 23 January 2018, https://www.todayonline.com/singapore/survey-finds-45-cent-singaporeans-unhappy-work-slight-improvement-last-year; Samuel Chang, "Singapore employees least engaged in Asia, study finds", *Straits Times*, 27 March 2017, https://www.straitstimes.com/business/singapore-employees-least-engaged-in-asia-study-finds.

ThinkThrough

It would seem that Boaz gets to meet Ruth "by chance" (Ruth 2:4). Do you believe in "coincidence" (2:4)? Why or why not? How can you discern God's hand in the events of your life?

In relating to others, what can we learn from Boaz in the way he relates with his workers, and how he treats strangers?

Day 10

Read Ruth 2:8–10, 13–16

Author Philip Yancey, in *What's So Amazing About Grace?*, tells of a comparative religion conference where experts from all over the world debated what, if any, belief was unique to the Christian faith. They began eliminating possibilities. Incarnation? Resurrection? But there are other faiths telling of deities that appeared in human form and also returned from death. The debate went on for some time, until theologian and philosopher C. S. Lewis joined the discussion. When told that they were trying to agree on the one unique characteristic of Christianity, Lewis responded, "Oh, that's easy. It's grace."[14]

Ruth has prayed that she can glean in a field where she will "find favour" or "grace" (Ruth 2:2 KJV). Grace is benevolence bestowed on one who doesn't deserve it and can't earn it. As an abject widow and foreigner, Ruth has no claims on anyone. Providentially, God leads her into a field owned by a relative of Elimelek (2:1, 3). Ruth now becomes the recipient of Boaz's undeserved favour (2:10, 13).

How is grace bestowed upon Ruth?

Boaz calling Ruth "my daughter" (2:8) tells us that he is a much older man, probably a contemporary of Naomi, for she too uses that term of endearment with Ruth (2:2). But I believe there is more. Boaz knows that Ruth has embraced Yahweh, the God of Israel (1:16). In addressing her as "my daughter" (2:8), he is acknowledging her as family; not a foreigner, not a Gentile, and certainly not an accursed Moabitess.

You and I, too, must marvel at the grace God has extended to us. As Gentiles, we were outside the covenant that God made with the Jews (Ephesians 2:11–13). But when we believe in Jesus, we are adopted into the family of God. We become sons and daughters of God (John 1:12).

Gleaners normally move from field to field, but Boaz asks Ruth to glean in his field only—and not only this one time, but throughout the entire barley and wheat harvests. Gleaners can move in only after harvesters have left an area, but Ruth is allowed to follow behind Boaz's workers (2:8–9). Boaz even orders his men to deliberately "pull out some stalks for her from the bundles and leave them for her to pick up" (2:16). Ruth is also allowed to drink the water Boaz provides for his workers, a privilege not normally permitted to gleaners. He even shares his food with her (2:9, 14). To ensure she is treated with respect, and not verbally abused or physically molested, he places her under his personal protection

(2:9, 15, 22). In giving her permission, provisions, and protection, Boaz is going beyond what is required by the law. Ruth has become the recipient of Boaz's extravagant generosity and abundant grace.

Ruth does not lose sight of who she is—a foreigner and someone even lower than a servant. Mindful that she is a recipient of undeserved grace, she asks to remain in that grace (2:10, 13). Likewise, may we in humility and gratitude pray like Ruth, "May I continue to find favour in your eyes, my [Lord]" (2:13).

[14] Philip Yancey, *What's So Amazing About Grace?* (Grand Rapids, MI: Zondervan, 1997), 45.

Would you agree with C. S. Lewis that "grace" is the one unique characteristic of Christianity? Why? How would you explain "grace" to a non-Christian?

How have you experienced grace this week? How did this unmerited act of kindness affect you? On whom can you bestow grace this week?

Day 11

Read Ruth 2:11–12

A modern fable tells of how a mother hen's sacrifice saved her young chicks: after a big fire, forest rangers began to assess the damage. One found a bird literally petrified in the ashes, perched statuesque on the ground at the base of a tree. Somewhat sickened by the eerie sight, he knocked it over with a stick. Three tiny chicks scurried out from under their dead mother's wings. The loving mother, keenly aware of impending disaster, had carried her offspring to the base of the tree and gathered them under her wings. When the blaze arrived and the heat scorched her small body, the mother had remained steadfast. Because she had been willing to die, those under the cover of her wings would live.[15]

Having noticed her presence in his field, enquired about her, and offered his protection (Ruth 2:5–9), Boaz now tells Ruth what he knows about her. Apparently, Ruth's loving devotion to Naomi and her radical commitment to Yahweh has earned her quite the reputation in Bethlehem (2:6, 11). His comments about her leaving home "to live with a people [she] did not know before" (2:11) are reminiscent of Abraham leaving his home in Ur "even though he did not know where he was going" (Hebrews 11:8, see Genesis 12:1; Acts 7:2–3). It would seem that Boaz is likening her faith to Abraham's. Her commitment to Yahweh is as radical and total as Abraham's!

Affirming her radical commitment to Yahweh (Ruth 2:11), Boaz prays that Ruth will be richly blessed by "the God of Israel, under whose wings you have come to take refuge" (2:12). **Boaz gives us one of the Bible's most endearing pictures of sacrificial love and divine protection: a mother bird protecting her young under her wings.**

Fresh out of slavery in Egypt, God's people were given a reminder of His protection: "You yourselves have seen . . . how I carried you on eagles' wings and brought you to myself" (Exodus 19:4). Celebrating God as his refuge, the psalmist assures us that "[God] will cover you with his feathers. He will shelter you with his wings. His faithful promises are your armor and protection" (Psalm 91:4 NLT).

This vivid metaphor affirms Ruth's faith in the God whom she has just embraced. A God who will spread out His wings to protect His own. God is her refuge. And ours as well.

[15] David Mikkelson, "Mother Bird Sacrifices Herself", Snopes.com, 2 December 2008, https://www.snopes.com/fact-check/a-wing-and-a-prayer/.

If, like Ruth, you have earned a reputation in your community (Ruth 2:11), what good or bad might people say of you?

Memorise Psalm 91:4. How does knowing God "will cover you with his feathers", and "shelter you with his wings" encourage and comfort you today?

Day 12

Read Ruth 2:17–19, 21–23

Gleaners would have to work very hard from morning to evening if they wanted to gather enough grain to sustain themselves and their families for the day. They lived day by day, and hand to mouth. Often, they gathered very little because unscrupulous land owners hindered access to their fields or harvested every bit of grain, even that which had fallen on the ground, leaving nothing for the destitute (Leviticus 19:9–10).

To provide for Naomi, Ruth diligently gleans in Boaz's field from morning till evening. Her diligence has already caught the attention of Boaz's foreman, who says, "She came into the field and has remained here from morning till now, except for a short rest in the shelter" (Ruth 2:7).

That evening, Ruth returns home with "an ephah"—about 13 kilograms (2:17)—of barley grain,[16] enough to last several weeks.[17] According to one Bible commentator, this was the equivalent of at least half a month's wages.[18] This large amount of barley is the result of Ruth's hard work. But it also means that Boaz's servants have helped her by obeying his instructions to deliberately leave some grain stalks for her (2:16). At mealtime, Boaz invites her to eat from his table (2:14), giving her such a large amount of food that "what she had left over after she had eaten enough" could be shared with Naomi (2:18). Ruth's abundance of food is the result of Boaz's kindness and grace.

Kindness begets kindness.

Grace given is grace multiplied (James 4:6). Ruth showed undeserved kindness towards Naomi. Commending Ruth's benevolence towards her mother-in-law, Boaz had prayed, "May the LORD repay you for what you have done", and assured her that she would be "richly rewarded by the LORD, the God of Israel, under whose wings you have come to take refuge" (Ruth 2:12). Now, Boaz becomes the answer to his own prayer. Both Ruth and Boaz demonstrate what "the Scriptures say, 'They share freely and give generously to the poor. Their good deeds will be remembered forever'" (2 Corinthians 9:9 NLT). Commending Boaz's kindness to Ruth and to her, Naomi now invokes a blessing, "Blessed be the man who took notice of you!" (Ruth 2:19).

Assured that Ruth has now come under the care and protection of Boaz, Naomi instructs her to stay in Boaz's fields "to glean until the barley and wheat harvests [are] finished" (2:23). This is the storyteller's way of showing us that for the next three to four months or so, Boaz and Ruth will spend many moments together, enabling them to grow in respect and affection for each other.

16 Footnote on Ruth 2:17 (NIV)
17 Note on Ruth 2:17 in Tremper Longman III and David E. Garland, *Expositor's Bible Commentary*, revised edition (Grand Rapids, MI: Zondervan, 2012).
18 Rubert L. Hubbard, *The Book of Ruth*, New International Commentary on the Old Testament (Grand Rapids, MI, Eerdmans, 1988), 50.

God wants us to be generous when it comes to helping the poor (see Deuteronomy 15:11). Do you consider yourself a generous person? Why or why not?

Are there poor people in your community? To whom is God is leading you to take notice of? How can you show kindness to them?

Day 13

Read Ruth 2:19–20

In some countries, laws have been enacted allowing aged parents to claim maintenance from their children. In Singapore, for example, the "Maintenance of Parents Act" gives neglected or abandoned parents the legal means to force their well-off children to support them financially.

In ancient Jewish society, there was a similar social safeguard in the Mosaic law. It stipulated how a well-to-do relative, known as a "guardian-redeemer" or "kinsman-redeemer" (in Hebrew, *go'el* means "to restore something to its original or proper state of existence")[19] was to help a destitute family member. **The "guardian-redeemer" is the great theme and central focus of the book of Ruth, and is first introduced here in verse 20.** It will be revisited in Ruth 3:9, 12; 4:1, 3, 6, 8, and 14.

When Ruth tells her how she had gleaned in the field of Boaz, a grateful Naomi invokes a second blessing on him: "The LORD bless him!" (2:20; see 2:19). More importantly, she acknowledges God's providence and covenantal blessings on her and her family: "[God] has not stopped showing his kindness to the living and the dead" (2:20). The Hebrew word *hesed* is used in the Old Testament to refer to God's covenant faithfulness

and loving-kindness. Naomi sees God behind Boaz's generosity. The same hand that once afflicted her (1:21) now blesses her.

Naomi tells Ruth why Boaz has so generously provided for them: "That man is our close relative; he is one of our guardian-redeemers" (2:20). Yes, Boaz is a close relative, one of many guardian-redeemers—but not the closest (3:12; 4:4). Although there is another relative with a far greater duty to care for Naomi and Ruth, Boaz has willingly, generously, and graciously taken on the responsibility of providing for Naomi and Ruth as if he is that closest relative. What a remarkable man!

The guardian-redeemer has various duties: to redeem the property of his kinsman and keep it in the family (Leviticus 25:23–34); to redeem a poor relative who has sold himself as a slave to an outsider (25:35–55); to seek out the murderer of his kinsman and bring them to justice (Numbers 35:9–34); and to marry a childless widow of a deceased brother to carry on his family line (Deuteronomy 25:5–10).

The concept of the kinsman-redeemer is applied to God in the Old Testament. God himself says He is the Redeemer of Israel no less than 18 times (e.g. Isaiah 41:13; 44:6, 24;

54:5; 63:16).[20] The New Testament tells of Christ our Redeemer, who gave "his life as a ransom for many" (Mark 10:45), "to buy freedom for us who were slaves to the law" so that we could be adopted as God's children (Galatians 4:5 NLT). Jesus, our Redeemer, our *go'el* who restores us, has made us right with our God (Romans 4:25).

[19] Footnote on Leviticus 25:25 in Tyndale, *NLT Study Bible*, 239.
[20] Katherine Harris, *Nelson's Foundational Bible Dictionary* (Nashville, TN: World Publishing, 2004), s.v. "redeemer".

ThinkThrough

What do you think about the concept of the kinsman-redeemer? Is the law of the kinsman-redeemer applicable today? Why or why not? If so, how would you carry out such duties today?

In what way is Jesus your kinsman-redeemer?

Day 14

Read Ruth 3:1–4

It is Naomi who raises the possibility of marriage for Ruth (Ruth 3:1). Jewish parents arranged marriages for their children (Genesis 24:3–4), which includes their daughters and widowed daughters-in-law. Naomi knows that there are guardian-redeemers in the extended family who can buy back Elimelek's property, provide for the widows, and continue the family line. Since love has developed between Boaz and Ruth, Naomi plans to make that happen. She is opportunistic. The problem lies in her chosen method of bringing these two together. **Perhaps Naomi believes that the ends justify the means.**

Everything about Naomi's plan has to do with Ruth's physical attractiveness (Ruth 3:2–4). Some commentators are careful not to infer any impropriety from this passage. But Ruth dressing up and being near Boaz after he has finished "drinking and was in good spirits"(3:7)—in other words, when he is under the influence of wine (reminiscent of Genesis 19:30–33 and 1 Samuel 25:36)—on the dirty threshing floor in the dark of the night all hint that there is something amiss here. The threshing floor was notorious for illicit sexual rendezvous during harvest time (see Hosea 9:1).[21]

Naomi's instruction, "Then go and uncover his feet and lie down"

(Ruth 3:4), is an interpretative nightmare for Bible teachers. Some take this literally: Ruth is to remove Boaz's blanket so that the cold of the night would awaken Boaz, and they could have a conversation about their future together. But each of the three Hebrew words used here ("uncover", "feet", and "lie down") have overtly sexual connotations.[22] In particular, "feet" is often used as a euphemism for genitalia in the Old Testament (Exodus 4:25; Isaiah 7:20; Ezekiel 16:25).[23] It would appear that there is nothing good or pure about Naomi's plan. Based on her instructions and the circumstance, location, and timing of this plan, some Bible scholars believe that Naomi is asking Ruth to seduce Boaz and commit sexual sin! We should not be surprised by this, as these are "the days when the judges ruled" (Ruth 1:1).

Even if Ruth doesn't, Naomi knows that Boaz is not the one with the greatest responsibility to marry Ruth. The word Naomi uses in Ruth 3:2 to describe Boaz is not the term she would have used for the closest relative. But if they are sexually involved, Boaz is legally bound to marry her (Deuteronomy 22:28–29). Even if we have misread her intentions, Naomi is not being "careful to do what is right in the eyes of everyone" (Romans 12:17). She does

not "abstain from all appearance of evil"
(1 Thessalonians 5:22 KJV). This secretive night
rendezvous, if discovered, would embarrass Boaz
and Ruth, tarnishing both their reputations.

As we shall see, Ruth and Boaz are quite willing
to be married. And that is God's intention too.
The question is, how? Will it be done God's way
or Naomi's scheming way? In trying to seize
opportunities, let us not manipulate people or
circumstances. It does matter if our methods are
unethical or biblically wrong. The ends do not
justify the means.

What do you think
of Naomi's plan
(Ruth 3:1–4)? Why
would you agree or
disagree with it?

If you were Naomi,
how would you have
approached this
matter of marriage
between Ruth and
Boaz?

[21] Note on Ruth 3:2 in Harris, Brown, and Moore, *Joshua, Judges, Ruth.*
[22] Daniel Isaac Block, *Judges, Ruth,* vol. 6, The New American Commentary
(Nashville, TN: Broadman & Holman comPublishers, 1999), 685; de Waard
and Nida, *A Translator's Handbook on the Book of Ruth,* 49.
[23] See footnote on Exodus 4:25 (NLT); Tyndale, *NLT Study Bible,* 132 ;
F. Brown, S. R. Driver, and C. A. Briggs, eds., *A Hebrew and English Lexicon
of the Old Testament* (Oxford University Press, 1952), 920; Bush, *Ruth–
Esther;* Block, *Judges, Ruth,* 685; Douglas K. Stuart, *Exodus,* vol. 2, The
New American Commentary (Nashville, TN: Broadman & Holman Publishers,
2006), 154–155.

Day 15

Read Ruth 3:5–9

In life, there are times when we have to make major decisions. You come to a fork in the road, make that one decision, and your life veers off in a completely new direction. For example, the decision to accept or reject Christ. To remain in your home church or leave. And, of course, whom to marry. That one decision determines everything else that follows. Christians who marry know they have to live with their choices.

Ruth has come to that point. She has carried out the first part of Naomi's plan and gone to the threshing floor (Ruth 3:5–6). But she chooses to do things differently, stopping short of any acts that would dishonour herself, Boaz, or the God she now worships.

At the critical moment when Boaz awakens, Ruth does not rub his feet or nibble his ear, or make any other seductive moves. Ruth does not use her sexuality to manipulate Boaz into marriage. Instead of appealing to his sensuality, she appeals to Boaz's godly maturity and sense of responsibility. **At a moment when emotions are running high, Ruth takes out the Bible and asks if Boaz would be willing to fulfil God's Word in her life.**

The Hebrew words translated as "spread the corner of your garment over me" (3:9), or "spread your wings over your servant" (ESV), is an idiomatic way of making a marriage proposal. When speaking of His relationship with Israel, God pledged His commitment to His people using the same idiomatic language: "I spread the corner of my garment over you . . . entered into a covenant with you . . . and you became mine" (Ezekiel 16:8). It established a marriage covenant that entailed protecting and providing for the wife.

Just as she sought refuge and put herself under Yahweh's "wings" when she came to Judah (Ruth 2:12), Ruth now seeks refuge under Boaz's wings with her bold marriage proposal (3:9). Ruth asks Boaz to marry her on the basis that he is a kinsman-redeemer (Leviticus 25:23–55), in accordance with levirate custom (Deuteronomy 25:5–10), to protect her and perpetuate the line of Mahlon (Ruth 4:10) by producing an heir.

This marriage proposal is altogether unprecedented in ancient Hebrew society. Here is a "servant" (3:9) asking the boss to marry her; a poor widow marrying a rich man, a younger woman marrying a man old enough to be her father; a Moabite asking a Jew to break ethnic, political, religious, and social taboos. From a human perspective, Ruth's proposal is a hopeless gamble, doomed from the start. But if God is writing the script and directing the drama, this is a marriage made in heaven.

Given that all the conditions were ripe for a sexual encounter, why was Ruth able to resist temptation? If you were in Ruth's situation, would you have chosen differently? In what ways would God's Word help (Psalm 119:9)?

Ruth proposed to Boaz even though that was not the social norm. What do you think of a woman proposing marriage to a man today? If you were a woman, would you do it? Why or why not?

Day 16

Read Ruth 3:10–13

In Shakespeare's *A Midsummer Night's Dream*, the young lovers lament about how true love will always face great obstacles, especially when those involved come from very different ethnic, cultural, and social backgrounds. The love of Ruth and Boaz is all these and more.

If Boaz was willing to marry Ruth (Ruth 3:11), why didn't he propose to Ruth in the first place? Perhaps, as some scholars suggest, Boaz, an older man from the same generation as Naomi (2:1), did not think that the much-younger Ruth would want to marry him. Perhaps he expected Ruth to marry one of the younger bachelors in Bethlehem (3:10). He may have concluded that he was out of the running. But he was mistaken.

There is a second obstacle, a more problematic legal impediment. The prevailing custom on levirate marriage gives the nearest relative the first right to marry Ruth (Deuteronomy 25:5–10). Boaz is only second in line (Ruth 3:12–13). There is a nearer relative in town, one with a stronger claim on Ruth and the property. As a man of integrity, Boaz has been waiting for him to act. Boaz will not violate the Mosaic law by jumping the gun. This obedience to God's law

reflects his submission to God. We see here another reason why Boaz is "a man of standing" (2:1).But since Ruth has forced the issue, Boaz will now approach this nearer relative and get him to decide quickly. Boaz is a man of grace. He is willing to be the kinsman-redeemer even though he is not legally obligated to do so (3:13).

In handling their relationship the proper way, Boaz and Ruth may end up losing it all: if the nearest relative exercises his right and marries Ruth, she and Boaz cannot be together. Perhaps seduction would have been quicker and more effective!

There is a lesson to be learned from this. **God's will must be done in God's way.** And God's way will keep us in God's will. God's way is that of obedience to His Word; it is dangerous and deadly to take shortcuts. But obedience to God can often be costly. Part of being wise and making moral decisions is learning to move responsibly, not recklessly. There is a real temptation for us to take the fastest and easiest option, even if it means breaking God's laws.

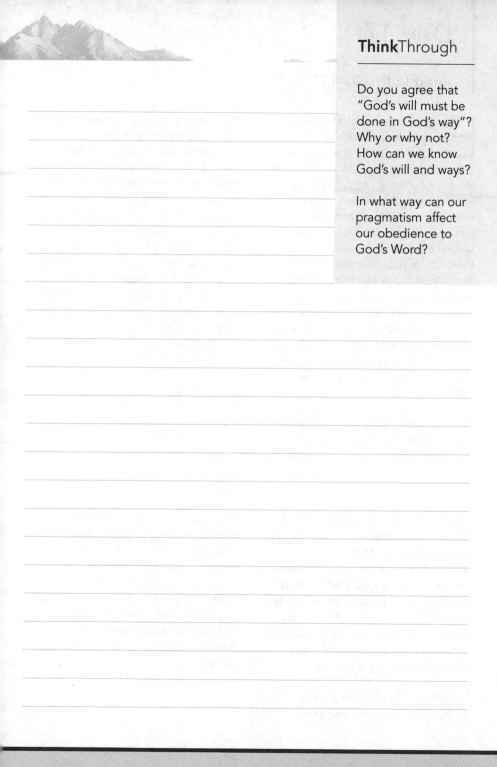

Do you agree that "God's will must be done in God's way"? Why or why not? How can we know God's will and ways?

In what way can our pragmatism affect our obedience to God's Word?

Day 17

Read Ruth 3:10–13

Every person has a different love story to tell. All love stories are unique and truly amazing. But the question in each story is the same: Whom would you marry? Well, we usually marry the person we are madly in love with. We find that special someone who fulfils the qualities that we believe our life partner should have. Quite naturally, we want one that is good-looking. But invariably, as Christians, we want someone who loves God, who is godly, and who is of good and Christ-like character. Some 30-odd years ago, I found the love of my life. And I eventually married my best friend Lay Keng, "a woman of noble character".

Grateful and greatly relieved that Ruth has handled the situation well and approached him in an honourable way despite the compromising setting, Boaz commends Ruth, "All the people of my town know that you are a woman of noble character" (Ruth 3:11). What attracts Boaz most is not Ruth's physical beauty; the Bible does not tell us what she looks like. **Instead, Boaz singles out her virtue and godly character.** In her short three to four months in Bethlehem, Ruth has garnered herself an excellent reputation. All the townsfolk have good things to say about her.

Literally, Boaz calls Ruth a *hah-yil* woman. The basic meaning behind this Hebrew word is "moral strength, good quality, integrity, virtue, comprehensive excellence". Hence, other English translations render *hah-yil* as "a woman of excellence" (NASB), "a worthy woman" (ESV), and "a virtuous woman" (NLT). This is the highest accolade anyone in the Jewish culture can give to a woman. This same Hebrew word is used to describe Boaz in Ruth 2:1 (see Day 8)—"a man of standing" (NIV) or "a worthy man" (ESV). Scriptures make clear that both Boaz and Ruth are godly people, thus making them a perfectly-matched couple for an exemplary marriage.

There are only two other occurrences of "a woman of noble character" in the Bible, and both are applied to the wife: "A wife of noble character is her husband's crown, but a disgraceful wife is like decay in his bones" (Proverbs 12:4); and, "A wife of noble character who can find? She is worth far more than rubies" (31:10). In describing the ideal woman and wife (31:10–31), King Lemuel is reminding us that what really matters is not physical but inner beauty. He calls us to honour "a woman of noble character", for "a woman who fears the LORD is to be praised" (31:30–31). My wife was such a woman. And so is Ruth.

Why are we more attracted to physical beauty than inner character? How can we learn to value inner beauty more than external appearance?

What kind of person is a "woman of noble character" (Proverbs 31:10–31)? What must you do to become a person of noble character?

Day 18

Read Ruth 3:14–15

I am saddened by the news that a highly respected author and apologist who has vigorously defended the Christian faith now has to defend his own reputation. He is embroiled in a personal lawsuit involving a married woman who sent nude photos to him. Admitting a lack of discretion and good judgment on his part, he concludes that he failed to exercise wise caution and guard himself from even the appearance of impropriety. He advises fellow Christian men to take extra precaution in their personal conduct and communications, especially with the opposite sex.

Boaz has awoken from a night of celebratory drinking to find himself in a potentially damaging situation, a situation that is ideal fodder for gossip and scandal. It is unsafe to send Ruth back into town alone and he himself cannot escort her home at that hour without inviting all kinds of questions. So he instructs Ruth to stay on the threshing floor until morning (Ruth 3:13). But he has to ensure that "no one must know that a woman came to the threshing-floor" (3:14).

As a man with moral scruples, Boaz does not take advantage of Ruth. Acting with great discretion, he takes judicious measures to make sure that no wild gossip tarnishes his own standing in the community (Ruth 2:1) or destroys Ruth's honour and reputation (3:11). As a man of integrity, Boaz will also not let this midnight incident become an excuse for the other, nearer relative in Bethlehem to not exercise his duty as go'el for Elimelek's family, even though that would be very convenient for himself.

Very early that morning, as soon as it is safe to do so, Boaz sends Ruth back home to Naomi. To keep their night meeting a secret, he does not escort her back to town. He then goes back to town by himself.

Naomi's scheme to bring Boaz and Ruth together needlessly put them in a compromising situation. She was not "careful to do what is right in the eyes of everyone" (Romans 12:17) and failed to "abstain from all appearance of evil" (1 Thessalonians 5:22 KJV), but did "what was right in [her] own eyes" Judges 17:6). Boaz and Ruth, however, did what was right in God's eyes (Acts 4:19).

As a man, I believe that I too am to be a moral leader in my relationship with the opposite sex. Naomi instructed Ruth to do whatever Boaz told her (Ruth 3:4). Had Boaz not been a man of character, the outcome would have been different. But Boaz took the high ground and assumed moral leadership. **Christian men need to exercise prudence**

and protect themselves from even the appearance of impropriety. More importantly, they need to help protect the purity and reputation of the women with whom they associate. This is what true spiritual and physical manhood is about.

If found together, who would likely get the blame—Naomi, Ruth, or Boaz? Why?

Why must we be "careful to do what is right in the eyes of everyone" (Romans 12:17)? Why is it important that we "abstain from all appearance of evil" (1 Thessalonians 5:22 KJV)?

Day 19

When you think about engagements, you usually imagine the exchange of rings between the couple as a sign of their future together. Engagement traditions differ from culture to culture. The Chinese include the sending of betrothal gifts to the bride's family on an auspicious day and reciprocal gifts to the groom's family. These gifts include jewellery, red packets containing money, household items (like bedding and even spittoons), and food (like wine, rice cakes, and pig trotters).

Ruth has proposed marriage to Boaz (Ruth 3:9). Though he wants to marry her, Boaz cannot accept the proposal just yet, as there is a nearer relative who has a stronger claim on Ruth. Boaz has to wait until the following day to ask this relative if he will marry Ruth or forego his right to do so (3:12–13).

Before he goes into town to seek out this man, Boaz sends Ruth back to Naomi with a generous gift: six measures of barley (3:15), or about 40 kilogrammes[24]—triple what Ruth gleaned on her first day in his fields (2:17).[25] The romantics among us would probably prefer an engagement ring or a bouquet of flowers. I suspect this hefty load of grain from Boaz is a symbolic gesture, albeit a certain and strong one, to reassure Ruth and Naomi that from now on, he is willing to take on the responsibility as *go'el*, guardian-redeemer. Given the circumstances, this is Boaz's version of an engagement ring.

The anxious mother-in-law, eager to know if her plan has been successful, asks Ruth, "How did it go, my daughter?" (3:16). In Hebrew, this question is literally, "Who art thou, my daughter?" Clearly, Naomi wants to know if Ruth remains Mahlon's widow or is now Boaz's wife.

In relating the events of the night, Ruth highlights that the barley is a gift from Boaz to Naomi (3:17). Naomi probably understands the significance of this gift. Assured of her desired outcome, she advises Ruth, "Wait, my daughter, until you find out what happens. For the man will not rest until the matter is settled today" (3:18). Naomi is confident that Boaz will see the matter through. Perhaps she knows that Boaz is a man of his word. Perhaps she is learning to see the Lord's hand in all this (2:20). **Her advice to "wait" reveals her renewed faith—a confident, expectant belief that only God can bring the venture to a successful conclusion.**

Part of being wise and making good and moral decisions is learning to move responsibly, not recklessly.

Too often, the call to step out in faith invites an impulse to act recklessly, with disastrous results. To wait is to do so in patient trust that God will act on your behalf. "Be still before the LORD and wait patiently for him" (Psalm 37:7) is the much-needed corrective to the pragmatic and the impatient in this fast-paced world. Wait. "Rest in the LORD" (37:7 NKJV).

[24] Note on Ruth 3:15 in Arthur E. Cundall and Leon Morris, *Judges and Ruth*, Tyndale Old Testament Commentaries (London: Inter-Varsity Press, 2008).
[25] Footnote on Ruth 2:17 in Barker, *NIV Study Bible*, 367.

ThinkThrough

How did God provide for you at a time of your greatest need (Ruth 3:17)?

What does it mean to wait patiently for the Lord, to "rest in the LORD" (Psalm 37:7)? Are you in a situation where the Lord is asking you to wait? How long have you been waiting? What can you do as you wait?

Day 20

Read Ruth 4:1–4

Having attended many weddings, I can't say I enjoy sitting through the all-too-familiar wedding ceremony. But there is one part of the ceremony that I actually do enjoy—when the couple shares with everyone the unique story of how they met, fell in love, and especially how they overcame the odds to be together.

The story of Boaz and Ruth has now reached a tipping point. Whether they will marry depends now on the decision of a third person, the nearer relative (Ruth 3:12–13). Boaz is not in control of the outcome.

Boaz is on a mission, a determined man. Wanting the matter to be settled quickly, he goes straight into town from the threshing floor, seeking out the man standing between him and Ruth. The "town gate" (4:1), the space between the town's outer and inner walls and their gates, serves as both town hall and courthouse. It is the centre of city life, where business and civil matters are settled in the presence of the town's elders (Deuteronomy 21:19; 22:15; 25:7; Proverbs 31:23, 31).

Boaz reaches the town square "just as the guardian-redeemer he had mentioned came along" (Ruth 4:1). This is not a coincidence. We have already seen how, "as it turned out", Ruth happened to glean in Boaz's field (2:3), and how, "just then" Boaz came to that same field at the same time (2:4). God's providential hand is directing the drama.

The kinsman-redeemer has two separate duties concerning Elimelek's estate. First, involving Naomi, he has to protect Elimelek's property (Leviticus 25:25–28). Second, involving Ruth, he has to marry Mahlon's widow to preserve the dead man's name and family line (Deuteronomy 25:5–10). Mosaic law does not command that the levirate marriage be carried out together with the property redemption. But Boaz asks the nearer relative to do both things, which seems to be the accepted and honourable practice of the day. By linking the two, the man must be prepared to assume a double financial burden. Perhaps Boaz wants to push the limits to see how far the nearer relative would be willing to go. Perhaps this is part of Boaz's negotiation strategy.

Boaz tactically raises the matter of land redemption first. Since Naomi does not have any more sons to inherit the property, the land will pass to the redeemer soon enough. Understandably, because it is to his financial advantage, the nearer relative immediately agrees to buy the property.

His reply, "I will redeem it" (Ruth 4:4), is bad news for Boaz. **As a man of integrity, Boaz has dealt with the matter in an honourable way.** Precisely because he wanted to do the right thing, he now finds himself at a disadvantage. Boaz now risks losing everything in this matter, including Ruth.

ThinkThrough

Boaz is determined to keep God's law (Ruth 4:4) even if it is potentially disadvantageous for him. Would you obey God's laws even though obedience would disadvantage you? Why or why not?

Did Boaz expect the nearer relative to assume the responsibility to redeem the land? Why or why not? What might Boaz be feeling when the man agrees to buy back the land for Naomi?

Read Ruth 4:5–6

Whenever we are asked to make a commitment involving our time, effort, or resources, we usually ask, "What's in it for me?" **This question is the subconscious mantra driving and directing many decisions we make.**

The nearer relative agrees to redeem Naomi's land because it is beneficial for him to do so. Redeeming the land at bargain prices is a fantastic opportunity. Naomi has no sons or grandsons to inherit the land, so the property will soon be his. Feeding an old woman will not take too much money, and it will not be long before she passes on. Even if he has to marry her, Naomi is past childbearing age. His redeeming the land would definitely be a profitable venture. Not only that, this good deed will also enhance his public image and standing in the community.

But there's more than just redeeming land. There are two widows, not one. Boaz reminds the nearer relative that it is a package deal of both property and posterity—of redeeming the family land and continuing the family line. Because he has to "acquire Ruth the Moabite" (Ruth 4:5), everything changes. The relative understands the implications. While the land is an asset, Ruth is a liability.

The relative considers the implications of marrying Ruth. First, he has to provide for Ruth and all the children from this marriage. Unlike Naomi, she is still young, probably younger than him. He will have to take care of Ruth for a very long time. Second, the first son born will be legally considered Mahlon's son, not his (4:10), and the ownership of this piece of land will return to Mahlon's family when this son comes of age. Third, this firstborn son will also be entitled to a share of this kinsman's own inheritance. And if this son with Ruth is the only one he has, then his own land will be inherited by Elimelek's heir, and his own name will die out. Fourth, Boaz deliberately highlights that he is marrying a Moabitess (4:5). Perhaps this nearer relative is a purist or racist, unwilling to marry a foreigner. Perhaps the fact that Naomi's two sons died after their Moabite intermarriage makes him reluctant to marry Ruth the Moabitess.

Redeeming a piece of land is good investment. But to assume family responsibilities for two widows, marry the foreign one, and let other people's children inherit the land he has just bought, would "endanger [his] own estate" (4:6). The nearer relative tells Boaz, "You redeem it yourself. I cannot do it" (4:6). I imagine Boaz shouting out loud, "Praise the Lord! My prayers are answered."

There are two positive outcomes. Firstly, the refusal of the other man to assume the responsibilities of a kinsman-redeemer only underscores the kindness and generosity of Boaz towards two needy widows.

Secondly, we can expect to hear wedding bells soon. Not all of life's stories will end happily like this one. But this episode reminds us that God is still writing the last chapter.

When was the last time you asked, "What's in it for me?", when asked to help out in church?

Is God asking you to assume additional responsibilities to care for your family? How would you respond?

Day 22

Read Ruth 4:1, 7–10

After recounting the story of Ruth in the Bible, the teacher asked his Sunday school class, "What's the name of the man who married Ruth?" Six-year-old Tommy confidently shouted, "Boaz!" The teacher then followed up with another question: "What's the name of the other man who didn't want to marry Ruth?" Another student shouted, "my friend!" (Ruth 4:1).

Conspicuously and curiously, the name of the other relative is never mentioned in this story. Boaz probably knew and would have called him by name. And his name would have been required for the transaction to be legal. But in telling this story, the author intentionally avoids naming him, or even providing any important details about him. The Hebrew words *peloni almoni*, rendered "my friend" (4:1) literally means, "so-and-so"! To convey the correct meaning of the Hebrew expression, the NET Bible calls him "John Doe" (4:1 NET)"—a name sometimes used to conceal a person's real identity.

Some scholars explain that the narrator wanted to protect him from the embarrassment resulting from his inability or unwillingness to assume responsibility for Ruth and Naomi. Rabbinic traditions, however, say that this is poetic justice for the one who refused to preserve the name of a kinsman because he was worried about his own inheritance and posterity.[26] So today, we don't even know his name!

Today, most transactions are formalised when parties sign on a dotted line in the presence of witnesses. But in the days of Ruth, "for the redemption and transfer of property to become final, one party took off his sandal and gave it to the other" (4:7). It would appear that by the time the story of Ruth was written, the exchange of sandals as a way of legalising business transactions was no longer practiced and hence, the editorial explanation provided in parentheses.

In the Bible, the feet also symbolises authority and ownership (Psalm 8:6; Ephesians 1:22). The removing of the sandal thus indicates that the unnamed relative is relinquishing all rights to the land, and the passing of the sandal to Boaz symbolises that Boaz now has the right to walk on the land as his property (see also Joshua 1:3; 14:9).

And we hear wedding bells. Boaz explains why he is assuming the responsibility of guardian-redeemer even though he is not legally bound to do so. Boaz marries Ruth "in order to maintain the name of the dead with his property", giving Mahlon a descendant "so that his name will not disappear from among his family or from his hometown" (4:5, 10). What selfless love!

With his part finished, the nearer relative, Mr "So-and-so", disappears into the pages of history, his name forgotten. **Today, we know only the name of Boaz, the generous and gracious kinsman (4:14) who acted with extraordinary covenantal love.** And, as an added bonus, we know Boaz as the ancestor of both Israel's most beloved king and the world's greatest King (Ruth 4:22; Matthew 1:5–16). Indeed, as the writer of Hebrews assures us, "God is not unjust; he will not forget your work and the love you have shown him as you have helped his people and continue to help them. We want each of you to show this same diligence to the very end" (Hebrews 6:10–11).

[26] Eskenazi and Frymer-Kensky, *The JPS Bible Commentary: Ruth*, 71.

ThinkThrough

What does Proverbs 22:1 say about the importance of maintaining a good name? According to Proverbs 3:3–4, how can we maintain a good name?

How does Hebrews 6:10–11 motivate you to continue to serve and help others?

Day 23

Read Ruth 4:11

Marriage is intimately personal, a sacred union between two individuals, a man and a woman. **But it is never a private affair; marriage must involve the community.** The couple would want the blessings of God and their community as they start a family. In many wedding services, the presiding minister will conclude with the congregation praying for God's blessings upon the newlyweds. I believe the communal approval and prayers encourage the permanence of the marriage.

Boaz asks the elders and townsfolk to be his witnesses (Ruth 4:9–10). But they take it upon themselves to pray for the couple too. Their benedictions include three very specific things (4:11–12). We consider two of these blessings today.

First, they pray for Ruth: "May the LORD make the woman who is coming into your home like Rachel and Leah, who together built up the family of Israel" (4:11). Their specific mention of Rachel and Leah, a reference going back some 900 years, is significant. Like Ruth, both had joined the Israelites from idolatrous foreign nations (Genesis 31:19–20). Rachel had been barren for many years before she bore children (29:31). Similarly, Ruth had been barren in Moab (Ruth 1:4–5).

Rachel and Leah gave Jacob the 12 sons from whom the nation of Israel descended. The townsfolk now pray that the Lord will make Ruth a fertile mother. In committing herself to Yahweh, Ruth has committed herself to God's people (4:16). The people of Bethlehem now fully accept her as part of the community. Henceforth, she is no longer called "Ruth the Moabitess" (1:22; 2:2, 6, 21; 4:5, 10). Instead, they elevate her to the same exalted status as Rachel and Leah—a member, a mother, and above all, a matriarch of their nation Israel.

Second, they pray for Boaz: that he will "have standing in Ephrathah and be famous in Bethlehem" (4:11). The use of "Ephrathah", Bethlehem's ancient patriarchal name, is significant, for the Hebrew word means "fruitful".[27] This is a prayer for Boaz's plentiful progeny. The marriage mandate has not changed: "Be fruitful and increase in number" (Genesis 1:28). Children are a blessing and not a curse; they are gifts from God (Ruth 4:12; Psalm 127:3–5; 128:3–4). Through our children, God is faithfully building our house. Like the townsfolk, we need to ask God to bless the family, for "unless the LORD builds the house, the builders labour in vain" (Psalm 127:1).

Boaz is already prominent, "a man of standing" (Ruth 2:1) known for his benevolent kindness. They now pray that he will become even more "famous in Bethlehem" (4:11).

God will answer their prayer in ways "immeasurably more than all" they can ask or imagine (Ephesians 3:20). Boaz's grandson, Jesse, will have eight sons, the youngest of whom will become the nation's most beloved and greatest king (Ruth 4:21–22; 1 Samuel 17:12)—David—from whom their Eternal King—Jesus Christ, their Messiah—is descended (Micah 5:2; Isaiah 11:10; Romans 15:12).

Boaz and Ruth are now famous beyond measure, for we are still discussing their story today. God himself established their house forever (2 Samuel 7:16; Psalm 89:4).

[27] Merrill F. Unger, *The New Unger's Bible Dictionary*, revised edition (Chicago, IL: Moody Publishers, 2006), s.v. "ephrathah".

ThinkThrough

In what way is marriage a community event? What roles can the church family play in your marital life?

If the elders of the church were to pray that "you have standing in [church] and be famous in [your community]", how would you like the church to remember you? What would you like to be known for?

Day 24

Read Ruth 4:12

Finding Your Roots is an American TV series that examines the family histories of well-known celebrities with mixed ancestry.[28] One featured celebrity guest, embarrassed to discover how one of his ancestors was a slave owner, admitted that "the very thought left a bad taste in my mouth".[29] Would Boaz, I wonder, be similarly embarrassed by his mixed lineage? His ancestors include a Canaanite prostitute (Matthew 1:5) and his forefather Perez was the product of a sexual scandal (Genesis 38:6–30). And now, as he starts his own family, it seems as though the townsfolk are deliberately embarrassing him with his tainted past by praying, "May your family be like that of Perez, whom Tamar bore to Judah" (Ruth 4:12).

Why would the townsfolk pray this?

Tamar was a Canaanite who posed as a prostitute to trick Judah, her father-in-law, into getting her pregnant (Genesis 38:6–30). Perez, the younger of the twin sons from this disreputable liaison (38:27–30), founded the Perez clan, the leading clan of Judah (Numbers 26:20–21) to which Boaz belongs (1 Chronicles 2:5, 9–12; Ruth 4:19–21). Perez was also the forefather of the Bethlehem clan (note "Ephrathah" and "Bethlehem" in 1 Chronicles 2:50–54).

There are many parallels between the story of Boaz and Ruth and the story of Perez's parents, Judah and Tamar (Genesis 38). Scholars believe that Perez was named here because of the *go'el* guardian-redeemer and levirate marriage issue involving Tamar. The story of Judah and Tamar is the most celebrated narrative of levirate custom. Tamar and Ruth, both foreigners, both young widows, participated in levirate marriages. God used both women to bear sons (Tamar albeit dishonourably, and Ruth honourably) to perpetuate a family line—the Messianic line—that was threatened with extinction.

Probably, most of the people praying this blessing on Boaz are themselves descendants of Perez. They are asking God to bless their kinsman who has acted faithfully to preserve their family line, by granting him a famous dynasty. God will abundantly answer this prayer. God is no man's debtor, and we can never out-give God (Romans 11:35 NLT).

Moabitess Ruth is not the only foreign woman in the Messiah's ancestry. God includes three others—Tamar (Genesis 38), Rahab (Joshua 2), and Bathsheba (2 Samuel 11–12) in the genealogy of Jesus (Matthew 1:3–6). **These women had messed up big-time, but their idolatrous or immoral past did not define them, for our gracious God included them in His plan to save the world.**

And with that same grace, He welcomes less-than-perfect persons like you and me into His family.

[28] "Finding Your Roots", PBS, accessed 21 September 2018, https://www.pbs.org/show/finding-your-roots/.
[29] "Ben Affleck: Sorry I hid the slave owner in my family tree", *TMZ*, 22 April 2015, http://www.tmz.com/2015/04/22/ben-affleck-ancestors-slave-owners-wikileaks-finding-your-roots/.

ThinkThrough

Four women of foreign descent and tarnished histories (Tamar, Rahab, Ruth, and Bathsheba) are ancestors of our Lord Jesus (Matthew 1:3–6). What does this tell you about who our God is?

How can 1 Timothy 1:15–16 encourage you not to let your past failures or sins prevent or deter you from serving our God?

Read Ruth 4:13

At the close of a recent wedding ceremony, the minister pronounced a benediction on the newlyweds. Concluding, he emphatically prayed that the couple would "be fruitful and increase in number" (Genesis 1:28), which immediately brought about an even louder chorus of "Amen" from the congregation. No pressure?

As a wealthy guardian-redeemer, Boaz can easily redeem the land for Elimelek. But he also marries Ruth. While in Moab as Mahlon's wife for 10 years, Ruth did not conceive (Ruth 1:4–5). The ancients attributed fertility and barrenness to God (Genesis 29:31; 30:2), as a barren womb was part of the covenantal curses (Deuteronomy 28:15, 18). If Ruth remains barren and cannot produce an heir, the family line is doomed.

Because God intervened and "enabled her to conceive, and [Ruth] gave birth to a son" (Ruth 4:13). This is the second time in this story that we read of God's direct divine action and providence (see 1:6). This baby is more than a product of sexual union between man and wife. He is "a gift from the Lord . . . a reward from him" (Psalm 127:3 NLT), and "the Lord's blessing for those who fear him" (128:4 NLT). God has answered the prayers for Ruth (Ruth 3:10) and Boaz (2:19–20)!

With the Lord opening her womb, Ruth has joined the ranks of women in the family line who conceived only because of divine intervention. At 90 and well past childbearing age, Sarah conceived and gave birth to Isaac, the son of promise (Genesis 17:17–19; 21:1–3). Similarly, in response to prayer, God opened the wombs of Rebekah and Rachel to give them sons (Genesis 25:21; 30:22).

These sons born to Sarah, Rebekah, Rachel—and centuries later to Mary (Luke 1:30–31)—tell the story of how God will keep his covenantal promise to Abraham: "I will make nations of you, and kings will come from you" (Genesis 17:4–6). That "the Lord enabled her to conceive" (Ruth 4:13) tells us that this son of Ruth is a continuation of that line of the many "sons of promise", and that kings will come from him. This son, as we will find out later, is the grandfather of Israel's favourite king David (4:21–22), from whom the Eternal King will come (Luke 1:31–33).

What God promises, He carries out (Numbers 23:19).

Joshua, confident that God will keep His promises, said, "Not one of all the Lord's good promises to Israel failed; every one was fulfilled" (Joshua 21:45). Paul would agree: "God will make this happen, for he who calls you is faithful" (1 Thessalonians 5:24 NLT). He is the faithful God who keeps His promises.

_____

_____

_____

_____

_____

_____

ThinkThrough

In the light of the Biblical mandate to "be fruitful and multiply" (Genesis 1:28), do you agree or disagree that Christians today should have more children? Why or why not?

Are children a blessing or a curse in our world today? Why?

_____

_____

_____

_____

_____

_____

_____

_____

_____

_____

_____

Read Ruth 4:14–17

My wife knew her days were numbered. The prognosis for her late-stage cancer gave her "a few months" at best. She was prepared to meet her Lord. One night, I asked her what was the one thing she wished she could do before she left. She said, "I want to carry my grandchild". Soon thereafter, she went home to her Father's house. Her wish remained unfulfilled.

Unlike my wife, Naomi's wish is fulfilled. Naomi gets to see her grandson, to cuddle him in her arms. In fact, she adopts him as her own son (Ruth 4:17).

The women—probably the same townsfolk who greeted a bitter Naomi coming home from Moab (1:19–21)—now celebrate the birth of Ruth's son with a rejoicing Naomi (4:14–15). Just months before, they had witnessed the widow's emptiness and bitterness (1:20–21). Now, they see her fullness and happiness because of the Lord's undeserved kindness and goodness. **They praise God for His faithful providence and benevolent provision.** In particular, they remind Naomi of two precious blessings from Him.

First, they praise God for giving Naomi another "guardian-redeemer". God has already provided the family with Boaz, but now He gives Naomi the additional benefit of another

go'el in this newborn. Doubly blessed, Naomi is assured that the family name will be fully restored. Their "praise be to the LORD, who this day has not left you without a guardian-redeemer" (4:14) turns out to be prophetic. From the lineage of this *go'el* will come the Redeemer par excellence, Jesus Christ (Matthew 20:28; Galatians 4:4–5), who will also be born in Bethlehem (Micah 5:2; John 7:42)—"the Saviour of the world" (1 John 4:14).

Next, the women remind Naomi what a precious blessing Ruth has been to her. They praise Ruth for her remarkable love and incomparable devotion to Naomi. For the first time in the story (Ruth 1:22), she is not called "Ruth the Moabitess" (the last time she was still referred to as such was in 4:10, just before her marriage to Boaz). For a society that values sons more than daughters, the accolade that Ruth "is better to [Naomi] than seven sons" is most exceptional (4:15). What this means is that Naomi, through Ruth, has received such great blessings as are normally supplied by seven sons, representing the ideal family. Ruth has received the highest compliment their culture can bestow!

Strangely, Boaz and Ruth do not name their newborn son. It is the townsfolk who name him "Obed" (4:17), which means "one who serves".[30] This is one of only two Old Testament examples where a newborn is not named by the parents or immediate family (Moses was the other—see Exodus 2:10). Obed was born to serve Naomi, to care for her in her old age (Ruth 4:15). And Obed, through his grandson David, will serve the entire nation (4:17; Psalm 89:3–4). And a descendant of Obed, the "one who serves", will become God's ultimate Servant (Isaiah 42; 52:13–53:12), who "did not come to be served, but to serve, and to give his life as a ransom for many" (Mark 10:45). That "[Obed] was the father of Jesse, the father of David" (Ruth 4:17) gives us a clue as to why this story is written. This we will consider tomorrow.

[30] Footnote on Ruth 4:17 in Barker, *NIV Study Bible*, 370.

ThinkThrough

Paul said that all who are in Christ are abundantly blessed (Ephesians 1:3). How has the Lord blessed you this past month?

Specifically, what is that one blessing that you are particularly grateful to have received from God? Why?

Day 27

Read Ruth 4:17–22

When she was in primary school, my youngest daughter was assigned a class project to trace her family tree. She came to me for help. Sadly, I was only able to identify with certainty family members of the previous two generations! When they were teenagers, my father and his older brother left their family in China to seek their fortune in Singapore, just after the Second World War. I have no knowledge of any relatives living in China today.

As he concludes this love story, the unnamed author of Ruth tells us that Obed "was the father of Jesse, the father of David" (Ruth 4:17). He also includes a genealogy of David, tracing his roots back some 900 years all the way to Perez (4:18). The fact that this is the family tree of David hints to us why this book was written.

As David is Israel's greatest and most-celebrated king, the author's purpose is to "introduce" him to the nation by recounting the humble lineage of their beloved king. The story testifies to how God watched over David's ancestors and guided them to fulfil His divine plan for the family, the nation, and the world. God providentially ensured that the Davidic line from which the Messiah comes would not go extinct (1:11–13). **The book of Ruth thus celebrates God's sovereign plan, power, providence, protection, and provision.**

The female townsfolk pray that Obed will "become famous throughout Israel!" (4:14). Their prayers are still being answered today. Every year, the Book of Ruth is read by orthodox Jews on the Feast of Harvest or Weeks, also known as the Feast of Pentecost, which is observed at the beginning of the wheat harvest (Exodus 23:16; 34:22). The Jews read this story at Pentecost because Ruth's marriage to Boaz was sealed during this festive harvest season, at the winnowing of the barley harvest (Ruth 3:2). And today, we are still reading and studying the story of his birth.

This genealogy reveals that David was of a mixed racial (Gentile) ancestry, and in particular, his great-grandmother was from the accursed Moablte race (Ruth 4:17–22). How do you think David as king of Israel felt to have his family secret revealed?

If you were to compile a genealogy of your family, how far back would you be able to go? How would knowing the stories of your ancestors enrich your life?

Day 28

Read Ruth 4:18–22

Once, I was asked to teach the gospel of Matthew to a Bible study group. I was given a lesson plan that began at Matthew 1:18; the first 17 verses were excluded. When asked about the omission, the organiser told me that there was nothing for me to teach since this passage is taken up by a long list of unfamiliar names. He didn't want me to bore the class with the lengthy genealogy.

What do we do with the many genealogical records in the Bible (e.g., 1 Chronicles 1–9; Matthew 1:1–17; Luke 3:23–38)? Many of us would skim through or skip them altogether. It's hard to see the relevance of these long lists of names.

However, since they are God's Word and the Holy Spirit has specifically included them, there must be something we can learn from them (2 Timothy 3:16). **Biblical genealogies tell us that God carries out His plans and purposes through real people living in the real world.** These names show that God cares about history, about families, and about individuals. They show that God uses imperfect people to carry out His plans and fulfil His purposes.

"This, then, is the family line of Perez" (Ruth 4:18). Perez's story is told in Genesis 38. We have already considered the scandalous past that plagued his birth, and the reason why he was mentioned in the prayers of the townsfolk (4:12, see Day 24). Besides the *go'el* guardian-redeemer and levirate marriage connection, there is a third reason why this genealogy is traced back to him.

On his deathbed, Jacob, Perez's grandfather, had prophesied that a king would come from this family line: "The sceptre will not depart from Judah, nor the ruler's staff from between his feet"; and that this kingly line will continue "until he to whom it belongs shall come and the obedience of the nations shall be his" (Genesis 49:10). Perez, Judah's son, therefore connects this prophecy concerning Judah to the love story of Boaz and Ruth. There will indeed be kings in the family line. Boaz and Ruth are the great-grandparents of King David.

This prophecy is still being fulfilled. The Davidic dynasty continues. The day will come when David's greater Son, "the Lion of the tribe of Judah, the Root of David", will rule the nations (Genesis 49:9; Revelation 5:5), when "at the name of Jesus every knee should bow, in heaven and on earth and under the earth, and every tongue declare that Jesus Christ is Lord" (Philippians 2:10–11 NLT).

The story of Ruth tells the story of King David, and the story of the King of Kings.

ThinkThrough

Do you agree that biblical genealogies are meaningless for Christians today? Why or why not?

How can you meaningfully apply this genealogy of David (Ruth 4:17–22) to your life today?

Read Ruth 4:18–22

Our names identify us. With more than 7.5 billion people in this world, it is my name that marks and differentiates me from the rest of humanity. My name affirms that I am an individual, unique, one of a kind. And my name tells a story—the story of my life.

Each name in this genealogy tells a story.

This genealogy also appears in 1 Chronicles 2:5–15, Matthew 1:3–6, and Luke 3:31–33. It includes 10 generations and spans some 850 years (1885–1040 BC).[31] The first five names—Perez, Hezron, Ram, Amminadab, and Nahshon (4:19–20)—cover some 450 years from the start of the Egyptian slavery to the time of Moses. The last five names—Salmon, Boaz, Obed, Jesse, and David (4:20–22)—cover 400 years from Joshua to the closing years of the judges.

As we have already seen, Perez was the son of Judah through Tamar (Genesis 38:12–30). Perez and his son Hezron were among the family of Jacob that went into Egypt (46:12). Nothing specific is mentioned about Ram (Ruth 4:19, 1 Chronicles 2:9).

Amminadab and Nahson were the father-in-law and brother-in-law of Aaron (Exodus 6:23). We are told that Nahshon was also the head and leader of the tribe of Judah (Numbers 1:7; 10:14; 1 Chronicles 2:10); rabbinic tradition credits him with exceptional courage as the first Israelite to enter the Red Sea. Only then did the waters part and the Israelites believe it was safe to cross.[32]

The Bible tells us nothing about who Salmon was or what he did, other than being "the father of Boaz" (Ruth 4:21). Matthew 1:5 says that Boaz's mother was Rahab, the Canaanite prostitute from Jericho. But Rahab is not Salmon's wife; she lived in Joshua's time, about 250 to 300 years earlier. Rahab was Boaz's "mother" in the sense that she was his ancestress, not his birth mother, in the same way that "Abraham is our father" (John 8:39).

Boaz is named "the father of Obed" instead of Mahlon or Elimelek. This is significant, considering that Boaz is supposed to produce an heir for Mahlon. Perhaps this is God's way of rewarding Boaz for his willingness to be guardian-redeemer. Jesse's story is told in 1 Samuel 16 and 17.

Every name has a story. We may not know the stories of people like Ram and Salmon. Their stories are not told to us. But they have been named. And God knows their stories.

You are named. And God knows your name. "But now, this is what the LORD

Read Genesis 38 and 1 Chronicles 2:1–13 to know Perez's story.

says—he who created you . . . he who formed you . . . 'Do not fear, for I have redeemed you; I have summoned you by name; you are mine'" (Isaiah 43:1). Redeemed and named. More importantly, God knows your story. In fact, He is writing it (Psalm 139:16).

What does it mean for God to summon you by name (Isaiah 43:1)?

[31] Note on Ruth 4:18–22 in John MacArthur, *The MacArthur Study Bible: NIV* (Nashville, TN: Thomas Nelson, 2013).

[32] Eskenazi and Frymer-Kensky, *The JPS Bible Commentary: Ruth*, 92–96.

Day 30

Read Isaiah 56:1, 3, 6–8, and Ruth 1:16–17

According to a recent news report, one in five Singaporean marriages in 2017 were inter-ethnic.[33] These mixed marriages were often inter-religious unions as well. The report highlights how parents generally expect their children to fall in love and marry people of their own race. Though mixed-race relationships are more common nowadays, such couples say that they still get strange looks in public and often face parental objections. Society is still not fully accepting of inter-racial marriages.

God warned the Israelites taking possession of the Promised Land not to intermarry with those already living there, for these unbelievers would inevitably lead them into idolatry (Exodus 34:15–16; Deuteronomy 7:1–4). The Moabites were such a people. Hostile to the Israelites, the Moabites hired the soothsayer Balaam to curse them (Deuteronomy 23:3–4). Their women seduced the Israelites into immorality and idolatry (Numbers 25:1–2). So God forbade them to enter the temple to worship Him (this law was still upheld at the time of Nehemiah, see Nehemiah 13:1–2, 23–27) and ordered the Israelites "never [to] promote the welfare and prosperity of the Moabites" (Deuteronomy 23:6 NLT).

This raises a troubling issue with Boaz the Israelite marrying Ruth the Moabitess. Did Boaz disobey God when he married Ruth? Why was Ruth permitted to join the Israelites and worship Yahweh?

In His grace and wisdom, God has already made efficacious provisions that allow anyone willing to believe in Him to worship Him. The prophet Isaiah promised that those who commit themselves to God would be bountifully blessed by Him: "Don't let foreigners who commit themselves to the LORD say, 'The LORD will never let me be part of his people'" (Isaiah 56:3 NLT). God promised them, "I will also bless the foreigners who commit themselves to the LORD, who serve him and love his name, who worship him, and who hold fast to my covenant. I will bring them to my holy mountain of Jerusalem and will fill them with joy in my house of prayer. I will accept their burnt offerings and sacrifices, because my Temple will be called a house of prayer for all nations" (56:6–7 NLT).

So, any curse on a foreigner or outsider alienated and separated from God lasts only until that person turns to God, believes in Him, and commits entirely to Him. And this is what Ruth the Moabitess has done (Ruth 1:14–18, see Day 6).

Ruth "turned to God from idols to serve the living and true God" (1 Thessalonians 1:9). And this is what we must do too.

The Ruth who married Mahlon (Ruth 1:4; 4:10) in Moab was an accursed Moabitess, not allowed to "enter the assembly of the LORD" (Deuteronomy 23:3), "excluded from citizenship in Israel and foreigners to the covenants of the promise" (Ephesians 2:12). But the Ruth who married Boaz in Bethlehem is now a "fellow [citizen] with God's people and also [member] of his household" (2:19).

Ruth was redeemed. Ruth was greatly blessed. This is the story of Ruth. You are redeemed. You have been richly blessed. And God is still writing your story. Amen.

[33] Toh Ee Ming and Joey Chua, "Mixed-race couples brave the odds for acceptance", *TODAY*, 10 August 2017, https://www.todayonline.com/singapore/mixed-race-couples-brave-odds-acceptance.

ThinkThrough

Does the Bible prohibit inter-ethnic marriages and inter-faith marriages? Why or why not?

What does God mean when He declares, "My house will be called a house of prayer for all nations" (Isaiah 56:7)?

Going Deeper in Your Walk with Christ

Whether you're a new Christian or have been a Christian for a while, it's worth taking a journey through the gospels of Matthew, Mark, Luke, and John. Each gospel presents a distinct aspect of Christ and helps us gain a deeper appreciation of who Jesus is, why He came, and what it means for us.

Hear His words. Witness His works. Deepen your walk with Jesus as you follow Him through the wonderful scenes painted in the gospels.

Our Daily
Bread
Journey
Through
Series™

✦ JourneyThrough™

Matthew

62 Daily Insights from God's Word by Mike Raiter

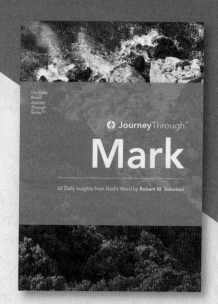

Our Daily
Bread
Journey
Through
Series™

✦ JourneyThrough™

Mark

62 Daily Insights from God's Word by Robert M. Solomon

Our Daily
Bread
Journey
Through
Series™

✦ JourneyThrough™

Luke

62 Daily Insights from God's Word by Mike Raiter

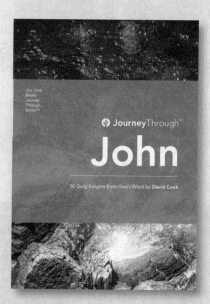

Our Daily
Bread
Journey
Through
Series™

✦ JourneyThrough™

John

50 Daily Insights from God's Word by David Cook

Journey Through

Acts

The book of Acts is one of the most exciting parts of the Bible. Jesus has just ascended to heaven, the Spirit has come to the church, and we see God at work building the church and causing the gospel message to spread through Judea, into Samaria, throughout Asia, into Europe, and finally to Rome. Embark on a daily journey through the book of Acts, and see how the Holy Spirit empowers the church to witness in ever widening circles until the gospel reaches the ends of the earth.

David Cook was Principal of the Sydney Missionary and Bible College for 26 years. He is an accomplished writer and has authored Bible commentaries, books on the Minor Prophets, and several Bible study guides.

Want to catch up on any back copies you may have missed from *Journey Through*? The series so far is available for purchase at

discoveryhouse.org.uk

For information on our resources, visit **ourdailybread.org**. Alternatively, please contact the office nearest you from the list below, or go to **ourdailybread.org/locations** for the complete list of offices.

BELARUS
Our Daily Bread Ministries
PO Box 82, Minsk, Belarus 220107
belarus@odb.org • (375-17) 2854657; (375-29) 9168799

GERMANY
Our Daily Bread Ministries e.V.
Schulstraße 42, 79540 Lörrach
deutsch@odb.org

IRELAND
Our Daily Bread Ministries
64 Baggot Street Lower, Dublin 2, D02 XC62
ireland@odb.org • +3531 (01) 676 7315

RUSSIA
MISSION Our Daily Bread
PO Box "Our Daily Bread",
str.Vokzalnaya 2, Smolensk, Russia 214961
russia@odb.org • 8(4812)660849; +7(951)7028049

UKRAINE
Christian Mission Our Daily Bread
PO Box 533, Kiev, Ukraine 01004
ukraine@odb.org • +380964407374; +380632112446

UNITED KINGDOM (Europe Regional Office)
Our Daily Bread Ministries
PO Box 1, Carnforth, Lancashire, LA5 9ES
europe@odb.org • 015395 64149

ourdailybread.org

Sign up to *Journey Through*

We would love to support you with the *Journey Through* series! Please be aware we can only provide one copy of each future *Journey Through* book per reader (previous books from the series are available to purchase).

If you know of other people who would be interested in this series, we can send you introductory *Journey Through* booklets to pass onto them (which include details on how they can easily sign up for the books themselves).

☐ **I would like to regularly receive the *Journey Through* series**

☐ **Please send me ____ copies of the *Journey Through* introductory booklet**

Just complete and return this sign up form to us at:

Our Daily Bread Ministries, PO Box 1, Carnforth, Lancashire, LA5 9ES, United Kingdom

Here at Our Daily Bread Ministries we take your privacy seriously. We will only use this personal information to manage your account, and regularly provide you with *Journey Through* series books and offers of other resources, three ministry update letters each year, and occasional additional mailings with news that's relevant to you. We will also send you ministry updates and/or details of Discovery House products by email if you agree to this. In order to do this we share your details with our UK-based mailing house and Our Daily Bread Ministries in the US. We do not sell or share personal information with anyone for marketing purposes.

Please do not complete and sign this form for anyone but yourself. You do not need to complete this form if you already receive regular copies of *Journey Through* from us.

Full Name (Mr/Mrs/Miss/Ms): _____

Address: _____

_____

Postcode: _____ Tel: _____

Email: _____
☐ I would like to receive email updates and details of Discovery House products.

Signature: _____

All our resources, including *Journey Through*, are available without cost. Many people, making even the smallest of donations, enable Our Daily Bread Ministries to reach others with the life-changing wisdom of the Bible. We are not funded or endowed by any group or denomination.